The Surname Tarratt

Susan Morris &
Wendy Bosberry-Scott

The question of surnames, their origins, distribution and history, lies at the heart of genealogy as well as being fascinating in its own right.

In the 1980s and 1990s, long before many genealogical sources were even indexed, let alone online, our Surname Report service provided expert assessments of the origins, history and distribution of selected British surnames, using the sources available at the time.

Now, with so many more sources available, we believe that these reports retain their value as studies of individual surnames, and so we are gradually making the Debrett Surname Archive available online and in print for the first time. Some modern indexes have been consulted to refresh and update the reports.

Debrett Ancestry Research Ltd, PO Box 379,
Winchester SO23 9YQ
Tel: 01962 841904
Email: info@debrettancestry.co.uk
Website: www.debrettancestry.co.uk

CONTENTS

Overview

The use of surnames in England began in the Norman period, when surnames were not necessarily hereditary but usually a form of description. Some described the individual's trade or profession; others were nicknames; some gave the father's Christian name; others gave the individual's place of residence or origin.

Different surnames might be used in different documents, or more than one surname given in one document. Early descriptions were fairly elaborate and by the thirteenth and fourteenth centuries these were simpler, but still variable, and indeed the instability of surnames continued until well into the seventeenth century.

Although some Normans would already have had hereditary surnames on their arrival in Britain, the passing on of a surname from generation to generation only became customary in Britain gradually during the course of the thirteenth and fourteenth centuries. At the end of this period most of the population apparently had surnames.

Variations in the spelling of a family's surname continue to be found until the present century. Before this, as most people could not read or write, the parish clerk or other official would write down the name as they heard it.

There are four main groups of surnames:

A - Local names, which describe a person by his place of residence or origin.

B - Occupational names, which describe a person by his trade or profession.

C - Surnames of relationship, which refer to the Christian name of the father or other important relative.

D - Nicknames or sobriquets, coined to describe a person in terms of his appearance or character.

Many surnames have uncertain origins, but the name Tarratt would seem to fall into the first of these categories, which is by far the largest.

Origins and Early Examples

C W Bardsley's *Dictionary of English and Welsh Surnames* (1901) states that the name Tarratt is 'doubtless a corruption of Tarrant'. His confidence would not be shared by modern scholars; recent research into surnames has found that detailed study in local sources often disproves the 'derivations' found in even modern surname dictionaries, because these were made on purely linguistic grounds. However, no alternative theory of the derivation of the surname is proffered by other scholars in any of the standard works, and so we have tested this theory in some detail.

Throughout the course of our research, relatively few references to the specific form Tarratt as such have been found.

M A Lower's *Patronymica Brittanica* (1860), an early but still valuable attempt to create a dictionary of British surnames, does not mention Tarrat(t) but gives the derivation for the surname Tarrant as 'a placename in Dorset'.

The late P H Reaney's *Dictionary of English Surnames*, which has been updated by R M Wilson, also lists Tarrant but not Tarratt.

In P Hanks & F Hodges' *Dictionary of Surnames* (1988), the surname Tarrant is described as a topographical name, given to someone who lived on the banks of the river of that name (the river Tarrant in Dorset). Hank and Hodges do not list Tarratt.

Eilert Ekwall's *Oxford Dictionary of English Place Names* draws upon a general survey of early and secondary sources including charters, deeds, the Domesday Book and maps, to chart the various early forms of a given place name and thus explain its meaning. Ekwall includes river names in his study and gives the following examples of the river name Tarrant:

Terrente	935
Terente dene	956
Tarente	1253

The same name, which is a variant of Trent, was also once the name of the River Arun in Sussex. The name has its origins in the British river name *Trisanton* which is a compound of *tri*, meaning 'through or across', and *santon*, a word related to the Welsh *hynt* (road) and the Irish *set* (journey). Ekwall suggests that the meaning appears to be literally, 'trespasser' and may have been used to indicate a river which was liable to flood.

The river name Tarrant has given rise to several place-names, all of them, except Tarrant Crawford, originally known simply as Tarrant. Tarrant Gunville, Tarrant Keynston, Tarrant Rawston and Tarrant Rushton took the names of the owner of the manor. Tarrant Hinton was owned by the *hiwan*, or inmates, of Shaftesbury Abbey; Tarrant Monkton was a manor held by the church of Tewkesbury. All these place-names, and Tarrant Crawford and Tarrant Launceston, follow the course of the river. Ekwall provides early references for

4

each of them but none of them appears in the form Tarratt.

The earliest noted example of the surname Tarrant is a reference to Reginald de Tarenta, who was mentioned in a Lincolnshire document in 1190 (F M Stenton, *Documents Illustrative of the Social and Economic History of the Danelaw*, London 1920). Other medieval examples of the surname are as follows:

1212	John de Tarent	Middlesex Curio Rolls
1272/3	Abbastissa de Tarento	Dorset Hundred Rolls
1296	Ralph Taraunt	Sussex Subsidy Rolls

The additional 'de', meaning of, in the Middlesex and Dorset names confirms the connection for these two men to the place name Tarrant.

A Calendar to the Feet of Fines for London and Middlesex 1189-1485, contains three further medieval references to Tarent but none to Tarratt, Terrett *etc.* (The feet of fines was a means of conveying or settling freehold property, from the reign of Richard I up to 1834, when a Statute was passed to abolish the method and set up a simpler way of achieving matters.)

> Adam de Tarent and Nicholas de Sancto Germano, six acres of land in Twikenham. And between the same Adam *[de Tarent]* and Richard Postell. Half a Virgate of land in the same village. And between the same Adam *[de Tarent]* and Richard Snel. Half an acre of land in the same village. Richard Snel calls to warrent Geoffrey Postell. John Anno 16 (1214)

5

Adam de Tarent and Geoffrey Postell. One Virgate of land in Twikenham. John Anno 16 (1214)

William abbot of the Monastery of the Blessed Mary of Grace next to the Tower of London and William bishop of Winchester, William Tarent, clerk and John Shordich the elder. The manor of Popellier held for life by Margaret, widow of Sir Nicholas Lorayne, knight. Richard II Anno 21 (1397)

The first two deeds refer to lands in the, then, village of Twickenham; the manor of Popellier refers to Poplar.

We can conclude from this survey of early forms that no medieval references of the surname Tarratt have been found, nor is there any evidence that the river or place name Tarrant was also found as Tarratt in early times.

In Ireland the name Tarrant has a different origin. In his *Guide to Irish Surnames* (1965), Edward MacLysaght states that the surname Tarrant is used in County Cork and that it is an anglicised form of Ó Toráin.

The following variants have been noted: Tarrant, Tarrent, Tarrat.

Distribution

In 1890 H B Guppy published his *Homes of Family Names in Great Britain*, a survey of surname distribution in Britain as a whole. His work was based on printed genealogies and a survey of county directories for the 1880s, in which he looked especially at the names of farmers, reasoning that they were among the least mobile groups in society. Guppy restricted his study to names which appeared in a proportion of 7:10,000 or higher. He did not mention the name Tarrat(t), Tarret(t), Tarrant, or Tarrent *etc*, indicating the rarity of the name(s) in national terms.

H R Moulton's *Palaeography, Genealogy and Topography* is a sale catalogue printed in the 1930s listing historical documents, ancient charters, leases, court rolls etc., which provides a further useful overview of surnames in England from medieval times onwards. There were no entries for the name Tarratt, but there was a reference to a John Tarrant, gentleman of Dorset:

> **28 November 1748 - Dorset**
> Exemplification under Seal of the Court of Common Pleas of the recovery suffered in Michaelmas Term 1748 between Ralph Phelps gent., demander and John Tarrant gent., and Robert Blumfield gent., tenants of four messuages and lands in Cranborn and Holwell co. Dorset.
> Vouchees: Joseph Neave and Elizabeth his wife, Edmund Wilson
> (Portrait of George II in initial letter)   30/-

7

Cranborne Chase is to the north west of the Tarrant villages; the town of Cranborne is to the north east. Holwell is further west. Clearly this Tarrant family had not moved far since medieval times.

Many of the sources available for charting surname distribution through the centuries are necessarily confined to the wealthier sectors of the population: in general, nobody wanted to know the names of the poor but the names of those with money or land were naturally of interest to the authorities. However, one source that covers the whole of the social spectrum is provided by English parish registers, the earliest of which began in 1538 following a mandate that all parish priests should keep a weekly record of all baptisms, marriages and burials that took place in their parish.

A survey of a cross section of parish registers for the years 1601 and 1602 was carried out in 1910 by F K and S Hitching; incidences of a particular surname are noted by parish and county, although with no indication of numbers of references. There were no references to Tarratt, Tarrett, Tarrant, Tarrent *etc*, again indicating a relatively rare name nationally.

A useful guide to the distribution of surnames for the sixteenth, seventeenth and eighteenth centuries in England is provided by the indexes to wills proved, and administrations granted, at the Prerogative Court of (the Archbishop of) Canterbury, in London, which had superior jurisdiction over local ecclesiastical courts where wills were proved until 1858. The PCC thus provides a national index, although it is not a completely representative one, as testators whose wills were proved in the PCC were mostly among the wealthier members of society, and a disproportionate number of them were from London or Middlesex and from the southern counties generally.

A search of the online indexes for the PCC found the following entries for Tarratt and its variants:

1429	Reginald Tyrett of Alington, Huntingdonshire
1588	John Tirrett of Forthampton, Gloucestershire
1628	John Terrett of Isle of Rey, France
1640	William Terrett
1642	Richard Terrett, yeoman of Chaceley, Worcestershire
1649	Thomas Terret/Terrett, yeoman of St Mary Margaret, Gloucester
1650	Elizabeth Terrett, widow of Forthampton, Gloucestershire
1686	Richard Terrett, mariner being bound to Guinea and other parts in the good ship called the Good Fellowship
1693	Michael Terrett, clothier of Horsley, Gloucestershire
1720	Isaac Terrett, Coachmaker of St James Westminster, Middx
1726	Thomas Terrett, blacksmith of All Hallows Barking, London
1752	John Terrett, cutler of Bristol
1755	William Terrett, yeoman of Owlpen, Gloucestershire
1760	Seth Tarratt, mariner belonging to HMS Dublin
1760	James Terrett, merchant, tailor of London
1761	Margaret Terrett, widow of St Anne, Middx
1761	William Terrett, mariner belonging to HMS Dublin

1763	George Tarratt , mariner belonging to HMS Prince
1766	William Terrett, baker of St Olave, Silver Street, London
1772	Thomas Terrett/Terret, cornfactor of Bristol
1773	Joseph Terrett, clothier of Uley, Gloucestershire
1776	Richard Terrett of Redmarley D'Abitot, Worcestershire
1780	Mary Terrett, widow of Redmarley D'Abitot, Worcestershire
1789	John Terrett, gentleman of Chaceley, Worcestershire
1805	Charles Terrett, paper hanger of Edward Street, Blackfriars Road, Surrey
1808	John Tarratt, hop merchant of Wolverhampton
1809	William Terrett, dyer of Ross, Herefordshire
1813	John Tarratt, hosier of Nottingham
1813	Mary Terrett of Bath, Somerset
1823	John Terrett, surgeon of Tewkesbury, Gloucestershire
1824	John Terrett of Hanley Castle, Worcestershire
1831	Mary Harris formerly Terrett, wife of Claines, Worcestershire
1836	Winifred Terrett, spinster of Bath, Somerset
1840	John Tarratt, merchant of Wolverhampton
1848	Joseph Tarratt of Bushbury, Staffordshire
1850	Jane Terrett, widow of Ross, Herefordshire
1852	John Terrett, hosier of Tewkesbury, Gloucestershire
1853	John Terrett, gentleman of Ruardean, Gloucestershire
1854	Octavia Tarratt of 10 Bedford Street, Bedford Sq, Middx

Most of these entries relate to testators in Gloucestershire named Terrett and this is by far the most commonly found of the variants of Tarratt. There is one appearance of Tyrett, which is also the earliest, in 1429 in Huntingdonshire.

The name Tarrant was found to be more widespread. One Tarrente was found in Sussex in 1612. Tarrant was found in Hampshire in 1630, Wiltshire in 1653, 1657, 1659, 1678 and 1687 and Middlesex in 1676. In 1653 in Wiltshire, the name was also noted as Turrant, and Tarran or Tarren was noted in Worcestershire in 1659. No references to the name Tarrant *etc* were found between 1694 and 1755, but between 1756 and 1800 Tarrant was found in Berkshire, Devon, Essex, Hampshire, Kent, Middlesex, Surrey, Warwickshire and Wiltshire. Four references were also found to Tarrants who died overseas, in 1693, 1757, 1762 and 1780.

The *International Genealogical Index* is an extensive (but by no means comprehensive) index to baptisms and marriages compiled by the Church of Latterday Saints, more commonly known as the Mormon Church. We used this index firstly to make a spot check of the counties in which the name Tarrant had thus far been found. If the two forms Tarratt and Tarrant were consistently found together, this would suggest that they are related. We found references to the name Tarratt (or variants) in each of these counties, with the notable exception of Dorset. Every county examined also contained references to the name Tarrant. The following list shows the earliest reference found in each county:

The International Genealogical Index (1992)
Berkshire
Tarrat(t) - nil
Terrett baptism 1685 - Great Faringdon

Devon
Terett baptism 1595 - Kilmington
Torrett baptism 1610 - Sidmouth
Tarratt baptism 1801 - Devonport

Dorset
Tarratt *etc* - nil

Essex
Tarrat(t) - nil
Territt marriage 1557 - Epping

Kent
Turrett marriage 1568 - Thanet
Tarrett baptism 1773 - Aylesford

London and Middlesex
Tarratt baptism 1693 - Stepney
Terrett baptism 1616 - Enfield
Territt baptism 1651 - St Benedict's Paul's Wharf
Tirrett marriage 1615 - Westminster St Martin in the
  Fields

Surrey
Terret marriage 1541 - Guildford
Tarratt marriage 1779 - Horsey

Warwickshire
Tyrret baptism 1706 - Lapworth
Tarratt baptism 1851 - Deritend and Bordesley

Wiltshire
Tarratt - nil
Tarret marriage 1765 - Chippenham

Worcestershire
Tarratt - nil
Tyrrett - 1593 - Bushley

The name was not found in great numbers in any of the counties we examined; the county with the largest number of entries for Tarrett or Terrett *etc* was Worcestershire. The most common spelling of the name was as Terrett. Other variations were Tarot, Tyrot, Tyrrett, Tearatt, Tirrett, Torrett, Terratt, Tarrett.

We found that the earliest occurrence of the specific form Tarrat(t) was in Stepney in 1693. This suggests that it is a relatively late variant.

We were interested to find large numbers of Terretts *etc* in Worcestershire and we looked more closely at the entries from this county. There were a good number of entries from the late sixteenth and seventeenth centuries and the earliest entries took the form Tyrrett.

We then looked at the IGI section for the adjacent county of Gloucestershire and again found a large number of Terrett entries (this was the dominant form, but the variant Tarratt was also noted). Again, the early references took the form Tyrrett. The name Tarrant was also fairly common in Gloucestershire and was found in some numbers as the variant Tarren.

Moving further south to Wiltshire, which bridges Dorset and Gloucestershire, we found many Tarrant entries but very few Terretts, all of them late. This would appear to confirm the supposition that Tarratt is more likely to be related to the form Tyrrett than Tarrant.

What, then, was the origin of the name Tyrrett that appeared in such numbers in Gloucestershire and Worcestershire? The name Tyrwhitt was noted in the Dorset section (a handful of nineteenth-century references from the parish of Winterbourne Whitechurch). This name, according to Reaney, comes from the Northumberland place-name Trewhitt (whose original form was Tirwit). We looked at the Northumberland section of the IGI and found over twenty references to the Tyrwhitt family in medieval times, but these were clearly taken from a secondary source (such as a published genealogy, or a family history supplied by a church member). We also noted, in Northumberland, several Terrot(t)s at Berwick in the eighteenth century.

An examination of the Yorkshire section of the IGI found more early Tyrret entries at Ripon in 1584 and 1597.

Reaney gives two pre-1400 examples of the surname Tyrwhitt:

1256	John de Tyrwyt	Assize Rolls, Northumberland
1383	William Tyrwhit	Inquisition Post Mortem, Gloucestershire

The first of these, as might be expected, refers to a man of Northumberland. The second, dated 1383, comes from Gloucestershire. If the source of the surname was solely the Northumberland place-name, then clearly this family had come a long way from Northumberland.

The titled family of Tyrwhitt is described in *Burke's Peerage and Baronetage* (1970). This traces the family back to John Tyrwhitt of Netherclay House in Somerset whose son Richard was born in 1772. Somerset is a long way from Northumberland, but close to Gloucestershire, home of William Tyrwhit in 1383.

14

The present baronetcy replaces an earlier title, which was created in 1611 and became extinct in 1784. This belonged to the Tirwhitt family of Ketilby or Kettleby, Lincolnshire, which features in *Burke's Extinct and Dormant Baronetcies* (1841). The entry in Burke's shows that the coat of arms of this Tirwhitt family incorporated three lapwings and the emblazon describes these as 'tyrwhitts, or lapwings'. The *Oxford English Dictionary* confirms that 'tirwhitt' is an obsolete name for the lapwing; the word is echoic, like 'peewit', and copies the cry of the bird. The source of this device would seem to be a legend published by the herald and historian William Camden in his history *Brittania* (1586) that a Northumbrian knight 'Sir Herculus', living in the year 1109, was severely wounded in defending a bridge, and that his companions were alerted to the location of his body by the screaming of a flock of lapwings, whose nests had been disturbed.

To summarise, in our study of the pre-1900 distribution of the surname Tarratt, we found no strong evidence to link the name Tarratt with Tarrant in Dorset, but more evidence to suggest that its original form was Tyrrett and that it was concentrated in Gloucestershire and Worcestershire by the end of the sixteenth century, when it was also found in Yorkshire. A link with the Northumberland name Tyrwhitt is not at all certain, but gentry families certainly moved around the country, as the lineage of the Baronets Tyrwhitt shows, and there was a Tyrwhitt in Gloucestershire in 1383. If we accept Reaney's derivation of the surname as coming from the Northumberland place-name alone, it would seem likely that a family or families from Northumberland moved south to proliferate in Worcestershire and

Gloucestershire in Tudor times, and that the name later took on forms such as Terrett and Tarratt. However, only detailed research into the history of individual families could prove such a link.

For the nineteenth century, H B Guppy's survey has been mentioned above. Another important Victorian source is the *Return of Owners of Land* of 1873, sometimes known as the Modern Domesday Book. This source lists, county by county, every owner of an acre of land or more, with their residence (not necessarily the address of their property) and the acreage of their holding.

Return of Owners of Land

(Berkshire	3	Tarrant)
(Buckinghamshire	2	Tarrant)
Gloucestershire	6	Terrett
Herefordshire	1	Terrett
Middlesex	1	Tharratt
Staffordshire	1	Tarrat
	3	Tarratt
(Wiltshire	2	Tarrant)

The highest concentration of the name in this list is in Gloucestershire where it was found as Terrett. Tarrat(t) was only found in Staffordshire and then only in small numbers; these entries probably refer to members of the family found in *Burke's Landed Gentry* (1937).

In Middlesex we found the surname Tharratt and this appears to be another variant of the name Tarratt; we returned to the IGI to look for Middlesex references in parish registers, but found very few entries; the earliest one for the name Tharratt was a baptism in 1728, and so this would not seem to be a significant form.

16

We found no references to either Tarrant or Tarratt etc in the *Dictionnaire de Noms et Prénoms de Franc,* (Larousse 1951), George F Black's, *The Surnames of Scotland* (New York Public Library 1946) or T J & Prys Morgan's, *Welsh Surnames* (Cardiff: University of Wales Press 1985). We did note from an American study of surnames that Tarrant, Tarratt and Terrett have all crossed the Atlantic and appeared in a Philadelphia directory in the 1850s.

A brief survey has been made of census records. The first decennial census return in England, Scotland and Wales was taken in 1801, but personal information was only recorded from 1841 onwards. The latest return currently open to public inspection is that of 1911 and all have been indexed by surname. We found the following numbers for Tarrat(t), Terret(t) and Tyrrett:

6 June 1841
Tarrat(t) (24); Tyrrett (1); Terret(t) (195)

30 March 1851
Tarrat(t) (16); Terret(t) (197)

7 April 1861
Tarrat(t) (34); Terret(t) (215)

2 April 1871
Tarrat(t) (37); Terret(t) (220)

3 April 1881
Tarrat(t) (112)l Tyrrett (3); Terret(t)(261)

5 April 1891
Tarrat(t) (51); Terret(t) (327)

17

31 March 1901
Tarrat(t) (88); Terret(t) (486)

2 April 1911
Tarrat(t) (157); Tyrrett (2); Terret(t) (511)

In 1841 there is just one showing of the name Tarratt in Wales, but ten Terret(t)s and one Terret(t) in Scotland. In 1851, the name appears in the Channel Islands (four entries) and Scotland (nine entries) as Terret(t), which rises to eleven entries in 1861 but drops down to one entry for 1871 and 1881. We see the name Terrett reappearing in the Channel Islands in 1891, but with (again) only one entry and this might indicate either a mis-transcription or a visitor to the islands during the time of the census.

For the years 1901 and 1911 there are surviving census records in Ireland (the earlier census returns were mostly destroyed) and the name Tyrrett appears twice in the 1911 index; Terret(t) appears 39 times in 1901 and 46 times in 1911.

Printed Genealogies

The only printed genealogy of a Tarratt family we have found is the entry in *Burke's Landed* Gentry (1937) mentioned above. We have found no published genealogies in standard sources for families of the names Tarrant, Tarrent or Tarrett *etc.* However, there are several published genealogies of Tyrwhitt (*etc*) families:

Tirwhit, or Tirwitt
Baker's Northampton, 1, 114
The Genealogist, v, 45

Tyrwhitt
Notices & Remains of the Family of Tyrwhitt (1858; 1862; 1872: London)
Appendix to Case of Sir J S Sidney, claiming to be Lord Lisle
Gentleman's Magazine, 1835, i, 154
Burke's Commoners, i, 583
Wotton's English Baronetage, i, 178
Burke's Extinct Baronetcies
The Genealogist, vi, 286
F C Cass, *East Barnet*, Part i, 26
Burke's Colonial Gentry, i, 211

Tyrwhitt-Drake
Burke's Commoners, i, 580
Burke's Landed Gentry

Heraldry

There are no coats of arms shown in Burke's *General Armory* (1884) granted to men of the name Tarratt but three coats of arms for families named Tyrwhitt are listed. One of these entries refers to the Tyrwhitt family of Ketilby (Lincolnshire) and Tyrwhitt (Northumberland). All of these include three golden lapwings on a red background.

Summary

It was not thought important until comparatively recently to be consistent about the spelling of surnames. The low levels of literacy, and the possibility that those persons keeping the records were 'imported' from another area of the country and therefore not familiar with the local dialects, meant that surnames, and even given names, could be spelled in a variety of different ways.

We have tested Bardsley's theory that Tarratt is a variant of Tarrant and while this cannot be ruled out, the evidence of distribution does not support it. What we have found suggests that the name might to be a late form of the name Tyrrett, which in turn may have its origins in the Northumbrian place-name and surname. However, the limits of this study make it difficult to be categoric about this and only detailed research into individual families bearing the name Tarratt would confirm this.

Sources Consulted

P H Reaney, *The Origins of English Surnames* (London: Routledge & Kegan Paul, 1967)

P H Reaney & R M Wilson, *A Dictionary of British Surnames* (Oxford: Oxford University Press, 3rd edition, 1995)

P H Reaney, *Dictionary of British Surnames* (London: Routledge & Kegan Paul, 2nd edition, 1976)

P Hanks & F Hodges, *A Dictionary of Surnames* (Oxford University Press, 1988)

M A Lower, *Patronymica Brittanica* (London, 1860)

C W Bardsley, *Dictionary of English and Welsh Surnames* (1901: reprinted, Baltimore: Genealogical Publishing Co, 1967)

C L'Estrange Ewen, *Guide to the Origin of British Surnames* (London: John Gifford, 1938)

H B Guppy, *Homes of Family Names in Great Britain* (London, 1890)

Ernest Weekley, *The Romance of Names* (London: John Murray, 2nd edition, 1917)

Ernest Weekley, *Surnames* (London: John Murray, 1917)

George F Black, *The Surnames of Scotland* (New York Public Library, 1946)

Edward McLysaght, *The Surnames of Ireland* (Dublin: Irish University Press, 1977)

T J & Prys Morgan, *Welsh Surnames* (Cardiff: University of Wales Press, 1985)

F K & S Hitching, *References to English Surnames in 1601* (Walton on Thames: Bernau, 1910)

F K & S Hitching, *References to English Surnames in 1602* (Walton on Thames: Bernau, 1911)

Debrett's People of Today (Debrett's Peerage Limited: London, 1996)

The Oxford Dictionary of National Biography (online, 2004–2014)

The Concise Dictionary of National Biography, Part II, 1901–1950, (Oxford, 1961)

Burke's Family Index (London: Burke's Peerage Limited, 1976)

H R Moulton, *Palaeography, Genealogy & Topography* (Sale Catalogue, 1930)

Index to Prerogative Court of Canterbury Wills (The National Archives: online)

G W Marshall, *The Genealogist's Guide* (1903; reprinted, Baltimore: GPC 1973)

23

J B Whitmore, *A Genealogical Guide* (London, 1953)

Charles Bridge, *An Index to Pedigrees* (London, 1867)

Geoffrey B Barrow, *The Genealogist's Guide* (London: Research Publishing Co, 1977)

Sir Bernard Burke, *The General Armory* (London, 1884)

C R Humphrey-Smith, editor, *Burke's General Armory Volume II,* (Tabard Press, 1973)

The Return of Owners of Land (1873)

Eilert Ekwall, *The Concise Oxford Dictionary of English Place-Names* (Oxford: Clarendon Press, 4th edition, 1960)

E G Withycombe, *The Oxford Dictionary of English Christian Names* (Oxford: Clarendon Press, 2nd edition, 1950)

W J Hardy & W Page, *A Calendar to the Feet of Fines for London and Middlesex: Vol 1 Richard I – Richard III (1189–1485)* (London, 1892)

Richard McKinley, *The Surnames of Oxfordshire* (English Surnames Series III: Leopard's Head Press, 1977)

Richard McKinley, *The Surnames of Sussex* (English Surnames Series V: Leopard's Head Press, 1988)

Richard McKinley, *The Surnames of Lancashire* (English Surnames Series IV: Leopard's Head Press, 1981)

Richard McKinley, *Norfolk and Suffolk Surnames in the Middle Ages* (English Surnames Series II: Phillimore, 1975)

George Redmonds, *Yorkshire West Riding* (English Surnames Series I: Phillimore, 1973)

The Norman People (London, 1874)

Debrett's Heraldry (London, 1933)

J P Brooke-Little, revised, *Boutell's Heraldry* (Frederick Warne: London, 1970)

Indexes to 1841–1911 Census Returns of England and Wales (The National Archives/*Ancestry.com*)

ScotlandsPeople: Indexes to Old Parish Registers, Testaments, Statutory Registers